Plans for
Small Gardens

A Wisley Handbook

Plans for Small Gardens

GEOFFREY K. COOMBS

Cassell

The Royal Horticultural Society

THE ROYAL HORTICULTURAL SOCIETY

Cassell Educational Limited
Villiers House, 41/47 Strand,
London WC2N 5JE
for the Royal Horticultural Society

First published 1975
New edition, fully revised and reset 1985
Second impression 1986
Third impression 1988
Third edition 1990
Reprinted 1991

British Library Cataloguing in Publication Data
Coombs Geoffrey K.
  Plans for small gardens.
  1. Gardening — Great Britain   2. Gardens
  — Great Britain — Design
  I. Title
  712′.6′0941   SB453.3.G7

ISBN 0-304-32002-1

Plans by Geoffrey K. Coombes
Photographs by Paul Roberts (Holland & Clark) and
Michael Warren

Phototypesetting by Chapterhouse Ltd., Formby
Printed in Hong Kong by Wing King Tong Co. Ltd

Cover: bird's eye view of a carefully planned small garden.
p. 1: plants of different heights, colours and foliage types can
be used to make the most of a narrow space.
Photographs by Andrew Lawson
p. 2: conifers and heathers combine to form an attractive low-
maintenance garden.
Back cover: a small paved area transformed with raised beds,
plants both in containers and on the wall, and a pool.
Photograph by Andrew Lawson

Contents

Introduction

It is wishful thinking to suppose that in a book of garden plans a design can be found to fit exactly into one's own plot and fulfil all the requirements of a new garden, or perhaps meet the needs and revised ideas for one long established. It is, however, likely that certain sections and features can be usefully applied from a ready-made plan or parts of several plans, such as arrangements for grouping shrubs and plants having regard for colour and spacing for specific purposes and places. The shape of a terrace for example could be taken in part from one plan and perhaps the outline of a border from another. Suggestions will be found for siting a greenhouse, garden shed and vegetables, all of which are common ingredients of many gardens differing in size and shape.

Opposite: A sink garden is a good way to grow small, choice plants.
Below: Steps can be planted with fragrant plants.

It is probably safe to say that many successful garden layouts, both on a grand scale and the smallest plot, started to take shape on a drawing board. The advantage of applying ideas to paper are manifold; one is that the whole area can be seen from a birds-eye view and gives a better idea of proportions. Another advantage is that different shapes of beds can be drawn and easily changed, paths put in position and eliminated at will, or the design of a terrace that appears to be wrong quickly erased.

I think that designing a garden is reminiscent of browsing through the glorious displays of a new seed catalogue in January, seemingly bringing the splendour of summer a little nearer. The similarity lies in the fact that when one begins the design the most uncompromising plot may be revealed as the garden of our dreams.

The basic essentials at this early stage are a measuring tape at least 60ft (18m) in length, a metal spike to secure the end (in lieu of someone to hold it) and a large writing pad. In addition wooden pegs, a straight edge, and spirit level are needed to establish levels; for larger areas boning rods may be required. These are T-shaped and consist of an upright leg about 4ft (1.2m) long and a cross member about 18 inches (45cm) long set at right angles at the top. A sighting is made by checking that the tops of the horizontal bar are in line.

It is worth spending a little time measuring as accurately as possible because one finishes with a plan that is to scale and recognizably similar in outline to the garden. The plan may be used to design beds in a specific shape and size, and to mark the position of other items in the design.

The drawing opposite illustrates a few principles for measuring a small area of land.

It is unusual for a plot to be exactly rectangular and the position of the house is not always parallel to the boundaries. By using the sides of the house as the datum and measuring by triangulation, the positions of the boundaries are established together with permanent features that have to be considered and eventually incorporated into the garden.

With regard to design I always follow the maxim that if it looks right on paper it will work out to a satisfactory conclusion on the ground. The drawing opposite shows how a shape can be accurately transferred to the site by using a boundary as a datum line and from this measurements are made at right angles at selected intervals to establish a curved outline.

Something should be said about 'shape' with reference to plant material. The outline of the borders and variations in heights produced by carefully placed specimen trees and shrubs at

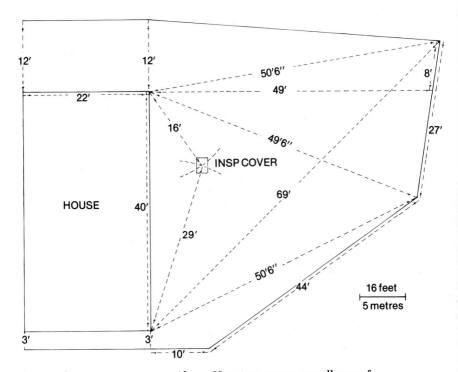

Above: How to measure a small area of land: the sides of the house are taken as a base for accurately measuring the boundaries and position of features on the site.

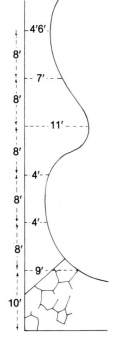

16 feet
5 metres

Left: Transferring a shape from the plan to the site: by using the boundary as a datum line measurements can be made at right angles at selected intervals to establish a curved outline.

Opposite: The enthusiast's garden at Wisley, one of a series of model gardens designed to show the potential of small plots.
Above: *Geranium endressii*, an attractive and useful ground cover plant for a position in light shade (see p.12).

certain places will constitute the framework for a design; an example of this, as a detail, is illustrated under 'Narrow gardens' (p. 31) by the simple shaping of a border and placing a narrow columnar tree towards the apex of the widest part of the bed which gives emphasis to a focal point.

Spacing is a vital technique. Shrubs and trees must be given enough space to grow, otherwise the plants will become over-crowded and shapeless. By advance planning, i.e. drawing the planting plan on paper to scale and allowing enough space for development, this situation can be avoided. When the plant first arrives it is difficult to appreciate that a shrub only 2 feet (60cm) high could increase to three times its size in three years. A nursery catalogue that gives the height, spread and flowering time to-gether with other information about plants will give a good idea of allowances to be made. For example if the total width of a phil-adelphus is 10 feet (3m), the space around the plant should have a radius of 5 feet. If the shrubs next to it in the bed will grow to 8 feet (2.5m) wide, the plants should be positioned 9 feet (2.7m) apart. This is of course a long-term solution, and by allowing enough room there is much bare ground round the newly planted shrubs.

There are several ways of bridging the interim period between planting and growing. The ideal way of making a garden look established from the beginning is in the use of ground cover plants. In the bare ground between the shrubs plant drifts and groups of carpeters that will make a complete ground cover without competing with the larger plants. The specimen shrubs may also be shown to better advantage by the plants underneath if carefully chosen for colour of flowers and foliage (an example of this is the scarlet-flowered *Rhododendron* 'Britannia' and *Saxifraga umbrosa*, the foam-like pink flowers of the latter combining well with the stronger tone of the rhododendron and the glossy green rosette of leaves making a dense carpet on the ground). Other easily propagated carpeters and therefore expendable are *Polygonum affine* 'Darjeeling Red' and 'Donald Lowndes' (see p. 37), *Stachys* 'Silver Carpet', *Geranium endressii* (see p. 11) and several cultivars of *Campanula*. Some of the plants that have been used primarily to cover the ground will be suppressed by the shrubs as they spread outwards but they will have made a most useful contribution to the border and in the open places some will remain and continue to grow.

Some shrubs make a much more significant feature if several of the same are planted close together in order to make one bold unit, for example *Ceratostigma willmottianum*, the small-growing shrub roses and hardy fuchsias. Depending on the size of the border many others can be planted in groups of three or more, the distances between the plants in a triangle being 18 inches to 2 feet apart (45 to 60cm) so that they join together making one substantial unit 6 feet acrosss (1.8m) in a shorter time than if only one is planted. This practice can be adopted throughout the planting scheme and in large beds shrubs such as *Cotoneaster salicifolius rugosus* could be 3 feet apart (60–90cm) but allowing 8 to 10 feet (2.6–3.1m) on the outer sides for development.

Most shrubs benefit from judicious pruning at some time, if only to nip back a wayward branch to maintain a good shape; for many others regular pruning is essential to obtain good results and has some bearing on spacing because, although in theory if a shrub is allowed to grow naturally it will attain a certain height and spread, its size can be contained by annual and careful pruning.

A typical example is *Buddleja davidii* cultivars which will eventually attain 10 to 15 feet (3–4.5m) with a gaunt open structure of branches, but by pruning hard in March a well shaped shrub within the space of 6 feet (1.8m) is maintained. Other shrubs that do not normally need hard pruning can also be contained within a smaller space than natural growth demands. It sometimes happens that with certain conifers and very large shrubs the spread of the lower branches exceeds the allotted space with the result that a view is hidden or access is obstructed. In some circumstances such conifers can be saved from destruction by removing the lower lateral branches up to 6 to 7 ft (2–2.25m) from the ground to leave a clean stem as shown below. If there are two or three main stems the branches can be removed in the same way making the tree in the shape of a standard with multiple stems. Shrubs that attain tree-like proportions respond equally well to similar pruning. The shrubby magnolias (see p. 14) are usually low branched in earlier years but eventually attain a height of up to 25 ft (7.5m), and if several of the largest ascending branches are selected and all other lower growth removed it is sometimes possible to have what is in effect a small tree in a limited space. The bay (Laurus nobilis) and Genista aetnenis, and in mild districts, Pittosporum are other examples of shrubs that can be treated in this way.

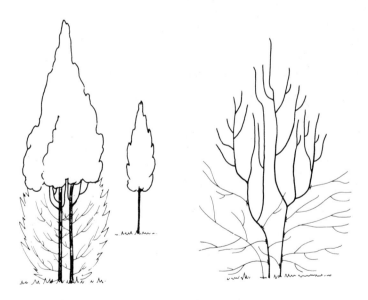

Access near a path or drive may be improved by the removal of lower branches from conifers and large shrubs.

Above: The magnolias provide a useful range of shrubs for the small garden. There are many different species and hybrids available, especially forms of *Magnolia* × *soulangiana* which is one of the most popular. Illustrated here is *Magnolia* × *soulangiana* 'Rustic Rubra'. Opposite: The 'family' garden - one of the model gardens at Wisley. This garden has been adapted from the plan on page 17, but the essential features remain the same.

A family garden

It could be said that the garden is a place of common interests, but diverse requirements, and sometimes the different needs are so many that it may seem impossible to include them all within a small space. There is, however, usually a common theme in the necessity to produce an attractive and colourful garden that is easily maintained, the latter being particularly necessary with a growing family which is inclined to make demands on free time at weekends.

The principal ingredients for a labour-saving garden are in many respects the same as those for any garden, consisting of flowering and evergreen shrubs, roses of all types and carpeting plants. But different age groups see the garden in different ways and those interested in climbing frames and swings for example will have little regard for the quality of the turf.

A sand-pit is often demanded by the youngest members of the family, and sometimes a place has to be found for a wendy house preferably in a sunny pleasant part of the garden and made a feature that is complementary to the whole design. Such a building has a relatively short life and it should be so arranged that after its removal the space can be planted and integrated with the rest of the garden.

Another feature is the children's garden where they can grow their own seeds and plants. This plot should occupy a favourable aspect and be likely to produce good results with little attention, otherwise the gardeners will be quickly discouraged. In Plan No. 1 the children's garden is shown with a continuous border 4 feet wide (1.2 m) and bordered with a paved path. This could be divided into smaller areas by paving at right angles to the main path to make beds 4 feet square (1.2 m²) which would be easier to maintain and different crops could be grown separately. It will be seen that the layout gives a good space for lawn and there is a dry hard surface from the house leading to the wendy house, sand-pit and vegetable garden. The borders of mixed shrubs and plants will give colour and interest at different times of the year, but bear in mind when making the choice that the young cricketer will sometimes score a boundary, and the goal-keeper will occasionally let a ball through right into the centre of a flower-bed. At this stage in the garden's development it may be better to plant tougher shrubs and plants in preference to the rare and

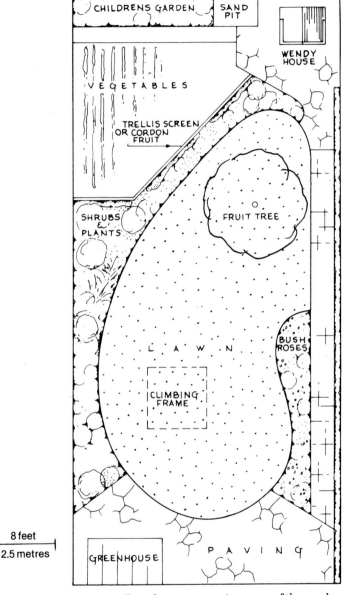

Plan 1: A design for a small garden incorporating some of the needs of a young family.

delicate. Roses can stand quite a lot of punishment from breaking; even pruning down into the old wood sometimes produces new growth from parts that have been dormant for some years.

17

Basically the design is very simple, the primary object being to provide a lawn that extends throughout nearly the whole length and breadth of the garden by introducing diagonal lines to the borders; it also provides space for shrubs and flowers. The screen which divides the vegetable section could be replaced with cordon fruit trees instead of lattice and ornamental climbers.

Concern is sometimes expressed (and not without reason) about poisonous seeds and berries and the injuries produced by some garden plants; the following list contains trees and shrubs that are commonly found in gardens. They should be treated with discretion but whether they are all eliminated from the garden is a personal decision. Berries and seeds to which children might be particularly attracted are marked thus*.

	Aconitum napellus	monkshood
	Aquilegia	columbine
	Buxus	box
*	*Convallaria*	lily-of-the-valley
*	*Cotoneaster*	
*	*Crataegus*	hawthorn
*	*Daphne mezereum*	mezereon
	Delphinium	
	Digitalis	foxglove
*	*Euonymus*	
	europaeus	spindletree
	Fritillaria meleagris	snakeshead fritillary
	Hedera	ivy
	Helleborus	Christmas rose
*	*Ilex*	holly
	Laburnum	
*	*Lupinus*	
	Narcissus	daffodil
	Papaver	poppy
*	*Prunus*	
	laurocerasus	laurel
*	*Sorbus*	rowan

Some trees and shrubs repel touch with an armour of needle-sharp thorns; to mention only a few, most of the *Berberis*, *Yucca gloriosa* (Adam's needle) and some of the *Pyracantha*, are examples. *Robinia pseudacacia* (false acacia) has a habit of dropping pieces of dead branch that bristle with large thorns, and *Hippophaë rhamnoides* (sea buckthorn), grown for its very attractive orange berries, has sharp spines.

Above: Monkshoods, in this case *Aconitum ferox*, have poisonous roots.
Below: The aptly named silver hedgehog holly, *Ilex aquifolium* 'Ferox Argentea'.

A plantsman's garden

The size of a garden has little to do with its quality and it is probably easier to maintain conditions of good cultivation in a very small garden than in a larger one.

The design in Plan No. 2 is the layout of a very small garden for someone who wants to grow a wide range of plants that need almost as wide a range of differing environments and includes raised beds, a pool, a greenhouse, a scree garden, climbing plants and shrubs. In this instance the raised beds are no more than 18 ins (45cm) in height and would therefore be little higher than some sink gardens. Good drainage is essential and preparation of the beds should be thoroughly carried out at the beginning. (For preparing raised beds see the Wisley handbook, *Alpines the easy way*.) It is intended that one of these areas is given over to rock plants and one or two miniature shrubs and conifers.

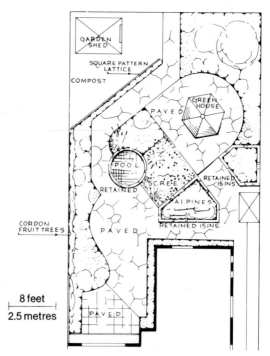

Plan 2: A connoisseur's garden, for varied interests.

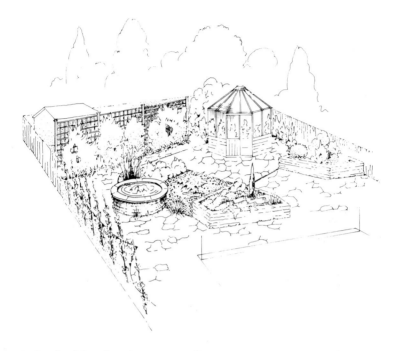

A sketch of the plan shown opposite.

The flat bed next to the pool is covered with shingle over which plants can scramble; the roots are established in the soil beneath and the stones drawn up close around the stems. The planting is not intended to cover the scree completely, and the colour of the stones should be appropriate to complement the plants and provide an interesting feature in contrast to the paving. The other bed near the pool is also at ground level and is suitable for small shrubs and low perennial plants. The pool is also raised to the same height as the retained beds and the coping around the edge offers a place to sit and watch activity in the water. In a small pool however the choice has to be made between plants and fish or a fountain because the turbulent movement of the water will not be welcome to either. I think it is better to have a fountain with a low projector for a small garden and it is worth while looking carefully at the different types on the market. There is for instance the fountain where the water emerges from the top of a tube as a thin descending veil shaped like a shining dome or a bubble fountain when a jet just breaks the water from under the surface. Without any fish or plants the water can be kept clean and even a little blue by the addition of copper sulphate.

Above: *Chamaecyparis pisifera* 'Boulevard', deservedly one of the most popular dwarf conifers.
Below: *Lithodora diffusa* 'Heavenly Blue' is a charming rock plant.

Hydrangea petiolaris is ideal for covering a wall (see plan 3).

Another raised bed offers a place for plants that will not thrive in the natural soil of the garden, for instance adding peaty, lime-free compost for dwarf azaleas or light gritty conditions for plants that will not thrive in clay soil.

The greenhouse is functional but also an architectural feature in any garden and ideal in a place where the more conventional shape cannot be partially hidden.

The cordon fruit trees (see also p.42) represent a collection of pears and apples and if the fences or walls along the boundaries are not suitable for more fruit the lattice screen is ideal for a fan trained plum. Alternatively soft fruit such as redcurrants and gooseberries could be trained as cordons against a trellis, including several different cultivars in a small space. The quality of the fruit grown in this way is generally superior to that produced in the usual way on bushes.

Plan No. 3 includes many features that the interested gardener might like to include and although the plot slopes up from the house the design could equally well be applied to one that is flat. The principal means of access to the garden is by the central steps which are wide enough to give a spacious and unrestricted feeling on approaching the lawn. A paved terrace at the highest part of the garden is reached by three steps of generous proportions and adjacent to this a rock garden is appropriately sited on ground

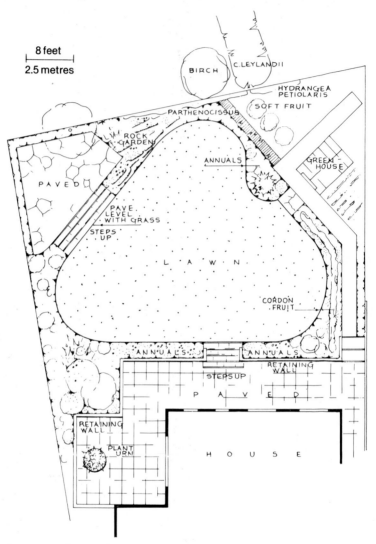

Plan 3: Another garden incorporating varied interests.

that is a natural slope.

In the opposite corner screened, by a low hedge of *Pyracantha* 'Watereri' there is a small area for soft fruit and salad crops and a greenhouse is sited with direct approach by a path from the house. The outline of the greenhouse is broken by a narrow conifer and cordon fruit trees that flank the path.

Opposite: lady's mantle, *Alchemilla mollis*, a beautiful perennial for the front of a bed (see p. 26).

Narrow gardens

The charm of a garden may be its seclusion, and in a very small space this is not always easily achieved. In a large garden a grass walk may lead to a hidden arbour or small lawn separated from the main part of the garden by a screen of shrubs. Plan 4 (opposite) shows a very narrow plot 19 feet wide (5.5m) that has been divided into two sections. The one nearest the house with a lawn is the largest and the other is hidden from view by hedges planted at right angles from the boundaries.

Having regard for the width of the garden, the height of the hedges would be the best set at about 4 to 5 feet (1.5m). Choosing a plant that can be trimmed close and compact is preferable to a hedge that is happier at twice the height. *Pyracantha* 'Watereri' is ideal and responds well to cutting, and *Cotoneaster lacteus* is equally good.

English yew (*Taxus baccata*) gives a look of excellence to a garden and forms a superb hedge particularly on chalky soil, but prefers not to be restricted below 4 ft (1.2m). For further information see the Wisley handbook *Hedges and screens* by F.W.Shepherd. Two important features about the design are the figure in the middle garden which gives a point of interest at the end of the path and is seen from the house and terrace, and the sundial, in the same section, which is visible from the paving in front of the summerhouse. Both objects are included to create focal points from two directions apart from an architectural function in the centre section.

The larger border that flanks the lawn could be planted with medium and small sized shrubs interplanted with two or three groups of floribunda roses. The narrow bed on the right side of the paved path might accommodate plants that like to sprawl such as *Gypsophila* 'Pink Star', *Nepeta* × *faassenii*, *Campanula poscharskyana*, *Alchemilla mollis* (see p. 25) and a few more upright ones such as *Lavandula spica* 'Hidcote', *Agapanthus* (see p.38) and *Cheiranthus cherii* 'Harpur Crewe'.

If, in the middle garden, the statue is raised upon a small plinth, the surrounding bed could be planted with plants that would partially hide the base of the stone. A suggested colour scheme is white and blue flowers, no more than $2\frac{1}{2}$ feet (75cm) high with grey-leaved shrubs. The L-shaped border behind the sundial provides space for numerous plants, depending on the size,

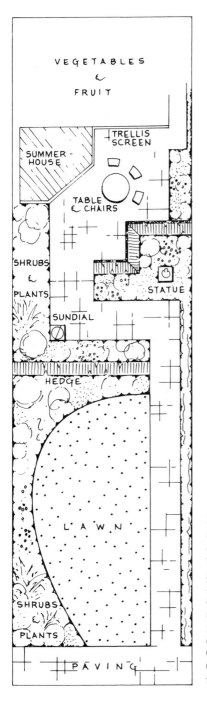

VEGETABLES & FRUIT

8 feet
2.5 metres

TRELLIS SCREEN

SUMMER-HOUSE

TABLE & CHAIRS

SHRUBS & PLANTS

STATUE

SUNDIAL

HEDGE

L A W N

SHRUBS & PLANTS

P A V I N G

Plan 4: Two gardens in one narrow strip. By dividing the garden with a hedge a secluded area is created, with the result that the entire garden cannot be seen from the house. This method of dividing the area into 'rooms' has been successfully employed in many gardens, large and small; for first-class examples see Sissinghurst Castle, Kent, or Hidcote Manor, Gloucestershire, both owned by the National Trust.

27

Rhododendron williamsianum, a delightful dwarf species.

conditions and aspect. In a cool lime-free soil a small collection of dwarf azaleas and rhododendrons interplanted with groups of lilies would be appropriate. Lilies are seen to advantage between low evergreens, the leaves of which seem to put the large blossoms into better proportion than the meagre foliage provided by the lilies themselves.

If rhododendrons will not grow some of the hardy fuchsias probably will, and the cultivars with large flowers which bloom from July onwards are 'Mrs Popple', 'Chillerton Beauty', 'Uncle Charlie' and 'Dr. Foster'. Earlier in the season colour can be introduced by interplanting with violets (see p.39) and dwarf bulbs.

At least some of the shrubs and plants near the sitting-out space in front of the summerhouse should be fragrant and the following cannot be overlooked; *Viburnum × juddii, Daphne burkwoodii, Lonicera americana, Jasminum officinale* 'Affine'. A few plants bedded out annually, for the benefit of their scent and worth the trouble are tobacco plants, heliotrope and ten-week stocks.

Above: Lilies, such as *Lilium lancifolium*, go well with rhododendrons.
Below: Jasmine should be planted where the scent can be appreciated.

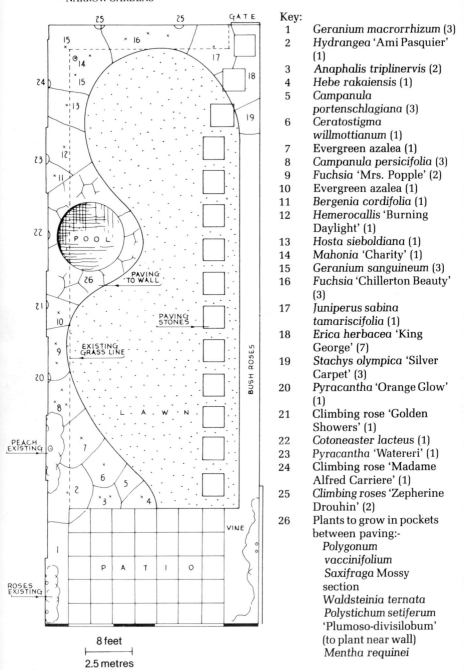

Key:
1 *Geranium macrorrhizum* (3)
2 *Hydrangea* 'Ami Pasquier' (1)
3 *Anaphalis triplinervis* (2)
4 *Hebe rakaiensis* (1)
5 *Campanula portenschlagiana* (3)
6 *Ceratostigma willmottianum* (1)
7 Evergreen azalea (1)
8 *Campanula persicifolia* (3)
9 *Fuchsia* 'Mrs. Popple' (2)
10 Evergreen azalea (1)
11 *Bergenia cordifolia* (1)
12 *Hemerocallis* 'Burning Daylight' (1)
13 *Hosta sieboldiana* (1)
14 *Mahonia* 'Charity' (1)
15 *Geranium sanguineum* (3)
16 *Fuchsia* 'Chillerton Beauty' (3)
17 *Juniperus sabina tamariscifolia* (1)
18 *Erica herbacea* 'King George' (7)
19 *Stachys olympica* 'Silver Carpet' (3)
20 *Pyracantha* 'Orange Glow' (1)
21 Climbing rose 'Golden Showers' (1)
22 *Cotoneaster lacteus* (1)
23 *Pyracantha* 'Watereri' (1)
24 Climbing rose 'Madame Alfred Carriere' (1)
25 Climbing roses 'Zepherine Drouhin' (2)
26 Plants to grow in pockets between paving:-
   Polygonum vaccinifolium
   Saxifraga Mossy section
   Waldsteinia ternata
   Polystichum setiferum 'Plumoso-divisilobum' (to plant near wall)
   Mentha requinei

8 feet
2.5 metres

Plan 5: A bold outline is one way of dealing with a long, narrow garden. Here, sweeping curves create interest, and a pool acts as a focal point.

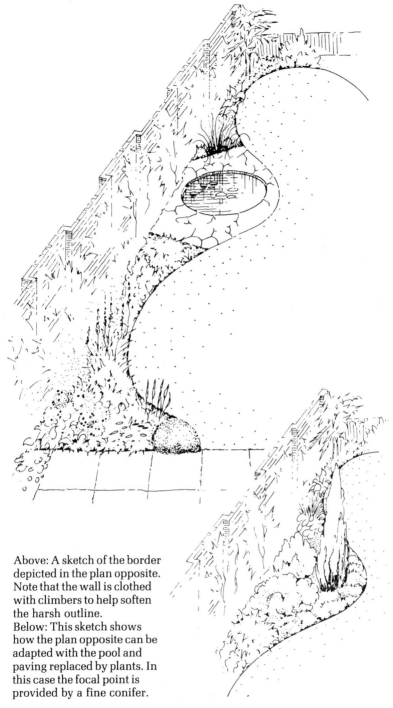

Above: A sketch of the border depicted in the plan opposite. Note that the wall is clothed with climbers to help soften the harsh outline.

Below: This sketch shows how the plan opposite can be adapted with the pool and paving replaced by plants. In this case the focal point is provided by a fine conifer.

Bergenia 'Silberlicht', one of many fine examples of these excellent plants.

Another narrow garden measuring 100 ft x 36 ft (30m x 11m) is depicted in Plan No. 5 (see p.30), and in this instance there is the possibility that the high wall on the left would appear out of scale to the width of the garden.

The flower border was originally straight and it has now been brought out into a deep curve from the wall and by contrast recedes back again towards the wall making the bed in places very narrow. The idea behind this is that the variation in shape helps to balance the relative height of the boundary.

One of the primary objects of the design was to include a pool which is formal to the extent that it is circular although it is in an informal context flanked with crazy paving and low-growing plants between some of the crevices. The border is a mixture of shrubs and perennial plants. Not everyone wishes to have a pool in the garden and one very good reason often expressed is because of the danger to young children.

The sketch on page 31 illustrates the same border with a narrow conifer at the widest part of it; a good variety for this purpose is *Chamaecyparis lawsoniana* 'Ellwoodii', which forms a compact blue-grey column. It is fairly slow-growing eventually attaining about 16 ft (4.6m) but it has advantages over some other, larger, conifers that might outgrow the position. An elevation at this spot

Mahonia 'Charity' has fragrant yellow flowers.

makes a focal point and has an influence on the garden design. It contrasts beautifully, for instance, with a carpet of winter- and summer-flowering heathers, or plants to give similar effect such as *Polygonum vacciniifolium* which will grow in a soil unsuitable for heathers.

A shrub that can also be used as an accent plant is *Mahonia* 'Charity' with a sturdy upright habit which reaches 8 ft (2.5 m) in height; the leaflets of the elegant foot long ash-like foliage give a striking architectural effect and in blossom it is one of the joys of early winter.

Plan No. 6 (see p.36) illustrates a design for a garden only 20 ft (6m) in width but with the use of curved and oblique lines the parallel boundaries are largely hidden. It will be seen that there too the paving near the house does not have to be straight-sided and the outline integrates with the garden.

The area near the plum tree is partly hidden and gives a feeling of seclusion, the arrangement of the lattice screen at right angles from the left boundary presents a direct view of the bed running obliquely across the garden.

Space for fruit is well represented and certain selected salad crops and vegetables could be grown.

Above: The model 'town garden' at Wisley.
Opposite, above: Arbours and statues create focal points.
Opposite, below: Day lilies are good herbaceous plants – this is
Hemerocallis 'Linda'.

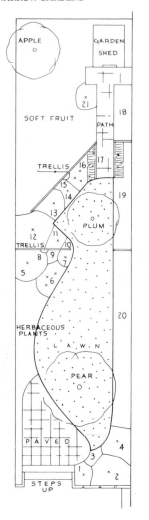

Key:

1   *Convolvulus cneorum* (1)
2   *Genista hispanica* (1)
3   *Anaphalis triplinervis* (3)
4   Hybrid musk rose 'Penelope' (1)
5   *Cistus cyprius* (1)
6   Floribunda rose 'Dearest' (3)
7   *Hebe albicans* (1)
8   Climbing rose 'Schoolgirl' (1)
9   *Campanula persicifolia* (3)
10   *Stachys olympica* 'Silver Carpet' (1)
11   *Ceratostigma willmottianum* (1)
12   *Spartium junceum* (1)
13   *Camellia japonica* 'Magnoliaeflora' (1)
14   Floribunda rose 'Iceberg' (1)
15   Climbing rose 'Sympathie' (1)
16   Polyantha rose 'The Fairy' (3)
17   *Lavandula spica* 'Hidcote' (10)
18   Herbs
19   *Fuchsia* 'Mrs. Popple' (6) *Campanula portenschlagiana* (6)
20   Low perennial plants
21   *Rosmarinus officinalis* (1)

8 feet
2.5 metres

Plan 6: A plan for a garden 20 feet (6m) wide. In addition to ornamental plants space has been left for fruit and herbs.

Opposite above: *Polygonum affine* 'Dimity', a useful carpeting plant.
Opposite below: Room can always be found for a striking foliage plant like *Hosta fortunei* 'Albopicta'.

Agapanthus produce striking blue flowers in summer (see p.26).

Above: *Lavandula stoechas*, French lavender, likes full sun.
Below: *Viola odorata*, sweet violet, a useful plant for ground cover.

Fruit and vegetables

In a very small garden it is doubtful if space-consuming vegetables, such as potatoes, are worth growing, and items that give a good return and occupy less room are to be preferred. Lettuce are easily grown and there is no comparison between one that is freshly cut and another that has had its growth terminated some time previously. It is also exciting to grow some of the less common items that are not usually seen in the shops, such as globe artichokes and sugar peas, and if you have a small greenhouse aubergines, tomatoes and sweet peppers may also be raised.

Runner beans have the great advantage of thriving on the same site from one year to the next provided the ground is fed. When runner beans are supported by a pyramid of canes or similar means, the blossom and bold foliage of the vines can produce an attractive elevation in the flower garden. The foliage of beetroot is sometimes a useful foil for flowers, while another plant with spectacular colours and delicious to eat is spinach beet which can be grown in flower borders or in the vegetable garden.

Apples and pears can be conveniently grown as cordons (a cordon is a form of tree trained to a single stem) when space is at a premium (see p.42), and a good position is often adjacent to a path where they receive light and air, and pruning and spraying can be done easily at the appropriate times. A judicious selection of cultivars should be able to provide the family with both cooking and eating apples throughout the winter and spring. Trained plum trees are usually grown against a framework of wires and canes or against a wall or fence. If soft fruit is grown, necessitating a cage, it might be preferable to put all the fruit under protective netting. An example of the fruit section of a small garden may be seen in the family garden at the Society's garden in Wisley (see p. 15). A diagram of the fruit and vegetable section of this garden is given opposite. For detailed advice on growing and harvesting fruit and vegetables see *The Fruit Garden Displayed* and *The Vegetable Garden Displayed*, both of which are published by The Royal Horticultural Society/Cassell.

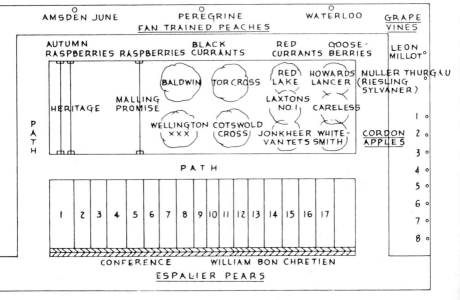

The fruit and vegetable section of the 'family garden' (see pp. 15 & 17).

Key (to diagram above)

Cordon Apples.
1. Sturmer Pippin
2. Ashmead's Kernel
3. Golden Delicious
4. Cox's Orange Pippin
5. Egremont Russet
6. Lord Lambourne
7. James Grieve
8. Red George Cave

Vegetables.
1. (Seed Bed)
2. Tomato 'Pixie'
3. Onion sets 'Stuttgarter Giant'
4. French bean 'Sprite'
5. Spinach beet 'Perpetual'
6. Salad onion 'White Lisbon'
7. Lettuce 'Unrivalled'
8. Beetroot 'Little Ball
9. Lettuce 'Fortune'
10. Brussels sprouts 'Peer Gynt'
11. Cabbage 'Hidena'
12. Carrot Nantes - Champion 'Scarlet Horn'
13. Parsnip 'Hollow Crown'
14. Courgette 'Green Bush F'
15. Cabbage 'Hispi'
16. Broad Bean 'Kordrin'
17. Potato 'Foremost'

41

Opposite: Cordon apples take up little space and produce a good crop of fruit; pears can also be grown in this way.
Above: Plants will grow in small pockets among paving stones.

43

Paved gardens

The gardens in many city situations are often very small and secluded by walls on all sides. It is usually preferable to keep the design formal although not necessarily employing a repetition of pattern, but one of balance. Plan No. 7 (opposite) represents a very small garden 28 ft x 28 ft (9m x 9m) and the beds are retained on three different levels, the small figure in the left corner being at the highest point.

Having laid down the basis of the design in the shape of the walls, which are of quite low elevation, one is left with a fairly flexible choice of plants and shrubs even if, as is sometimes the case, the garden is shaded by buildings. In locations such as these

Good use made of walls in a small garden.

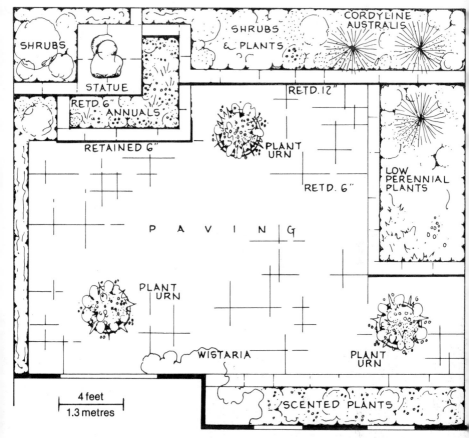

Plan 7: In a tiny area greater interest is introduced by beds on different levels. This garden measures 28 × 24 ft (8.5 × 7m); focal points are created both architecturally and with plants.

the temperature is often several degrees higher than in the open countryside and some less hardy and unusual plants thrive happily. Interest through the year can be maintained with foliage of different colour and texture, low perennials, annuals and bulbs.

The introduction of a formal pool is shown in Plan No. 8 (see pp. 48 & 49) in a different context and the intention is to fit it into the concept of a semi-naturalized garden and relate it to the existing paving.

In this case, it was useless to try and match the weathered stone that had been down for some years and therefore broken paving was used to unify adverse composition of material and pattern. Both plans produce the same objective but one is for a smaller layout and the same features are represented in each.

45

Above: *Convolvulus cneorum*, rue, and ivy mingle well together.
Opposite: Pink, blue and silver creates an effective colour scheme.

Below and opposite above: Plan 8, two versions. Designs for relating a
formal pool to an existing patio in a naturalized garden (see p.45).
In this case broken paving was used to match the stone that was already
in situ, but it should be remembered that a very wide range of paving
materials exists today. Examples to choose from include bricks (of many
different types and colours), concrete, stone, reconstituted stone and
gravel of different grades.

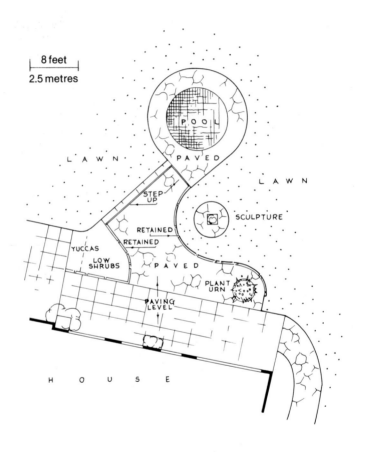

8 feet
2.5 metres

POOL

LAWN

PAVED

LAWN

STEP UP

SCULPTURE

RETAINED

RETAINED

YUCCAS

LOW SHRUBS

PAVED

PLANT URN

PAVING LEVEL

H O U S E

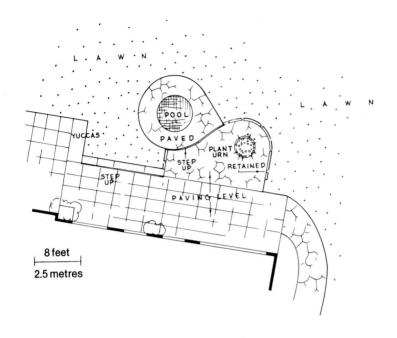

Below: Sketch of the pool featured in the plan opposite.

Corner sites

The usual characteristic of most corner sites is to see a boundary line running obliquely across the view and in this case, as in other gardens, we should try to take advantage of the longest aspect which in these situations is towards the point where the boundaries meet.

In Plan No. 9 (below) I have produced a lawn that takes almost

Plan 9: A corner site with a large lawn.

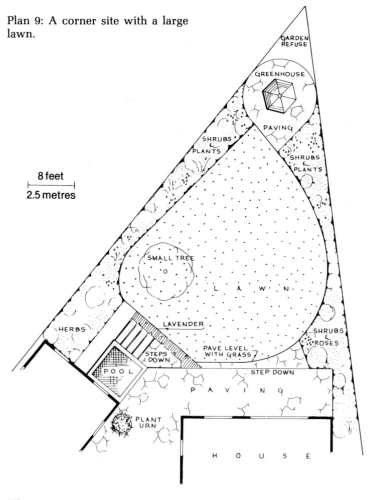

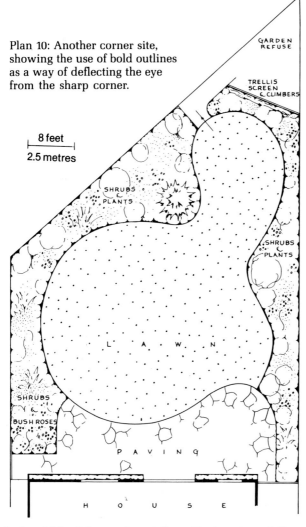

Plan 10: Another corner site, showing the use of bold outlines as a way of deflecting the eye from the sharp corner.

GARDEN REFUSE

TRELLIS SCREEN & CLIMBERS

8 feet

2.5 metres

SHRUBS & PLANTS

SHRUBS & PLANTS

L A W N

SHRUBS & BUSH ROSES

P A V I N q

H O U S E

the whole width of the garden at the widest part, and diverted the eye towards the architectural structure of a hexagonal greenhouse and away from the boundary that runs obliquely across the view. The small tree on the left side also deflects the eye towards the right.

Plan No. 10 (above) also illustrates a similar situation but designed with a somewhat different approach. The line of the paving near the house is part of a continuous outline of the lawn which extends in a deep curve to a prominent convex curve towards the centre of the garden. The apex of the bed is given emphasis by an upright shrub or small tree or an architectural feature and the storage space and garden refuse is screened with panels of square lattice up which climbing plants can be grown.

Three different gardens

The gardens represented in Plans No. 11, 12 and 13 incorporate features that are common to the needs of many gardens. The first plan (below) is that of a garden above the patio and the higher ground is retained by a low wall 2 ft (60cm) in height with access

Plan 11: Paved areas and a lawn.

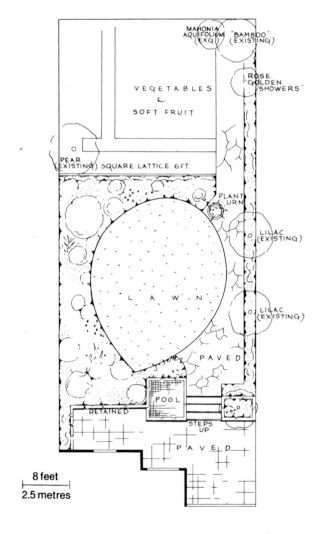

to it by four steps. If water is to be part of the design I think this situation is ideal for a formal raised pool, retained by the wall at the front, level with the soil and with paving at the back and sides. This allows plants to grow over the edges and the pool is close enough to the house for the pond life to be enjoyed even from indoors. The paved area above the steps gives a feeling of spaciousness combined with the lawn and adds further room for tables and chairs.

The garden depicted in Plan 12 (see p.54) is relatively narrow compared with the length, 25 feet (7.6m). Specific focal points have been created to distract the eye from a view straight down the garden; a curved path and divided lawn help to disguise the long, narrow nature of the plot.

In a shaded patio at the side of the house, plant containers hold foliage plants that include *Fatsia japonica*, *Euonymus fortunei radicans* 'Silver Queen', dwarf *Arundinaria* and *Phormium*, whilst blossom is contributed by *Impatiens* and *Begonia semperflorens*. Also near the house a pool is balanced by a plant urn on the opposite side with an accent of colour provided by spring and summer flowers. A fountain is well placed either as a single jet or bell fountain in the centre of the pool. About half way down the garden on the left side a birdbath emphasises the apex of the border and the lawn at this point narrows to 8 feet (2.5m) wide before terminating at a screen of climbing plants to hide the vegetable section and buildings beyond.

When the garden is a foot or two above the ground floor of the house, as it is in Plan No. 13 (see p.55), the basic layout and plant material needs careful consideration. In this garden the existing retaining wall was a short distance from the windows and constructed straight across from one side to the other and gave a feeling that it was inadequate to prevent the garden encroaching towards the house.

To modify this impression the design is aligned in one direction and the patio shape is altered by changing the line of the wall; the actual area of paving remains about the same by taking a corner off the lower right side and extending it on the left to produce a longer view of the patio in this direction. The choice of shrubs and plants is important in a garden that is on a higher level or a garden that slopes upwards away from the house. It becomes apparent that, for example, upright bush roses or some of the taller perennials when planted too near a house, not only obscure the garden but also ensure that the most visible part of the plants is the lower part of the stems with the result that the effect of the flowers is lost. Taller planting on the sides, leaving the centre open, would form a framework for the rest of the garden.

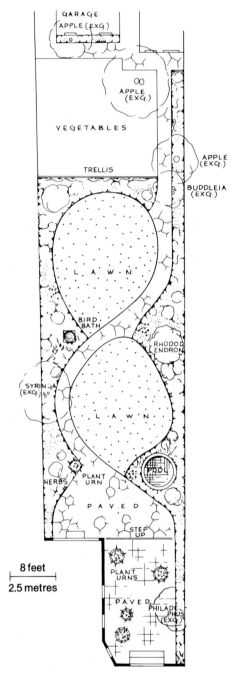

Plan 12: A garden designed for easy access (see p. 53).

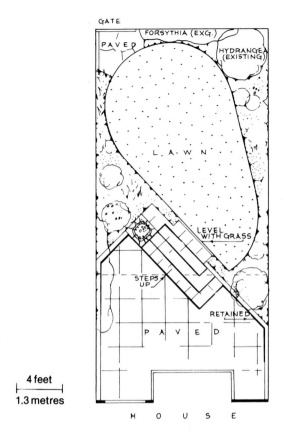

GATE

FORSYTHIA (EXG.)

PAVED

HYDRANGEA (EXISTING)

L A W N

LEVEL WITH GRASS

STEPS UP

RETAINED

P A V E D

4 feet

1.3 metres

H O U S E

Above: Plan 13 makes use of oblique angles to give an appearance of space (see p. 53).
Below: A sketch showing the effect created by the plan above.

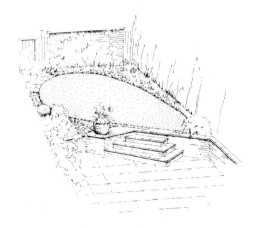

A north-facing garden

Except on particularly hot days in summer, sitting on a permanently shady side of the house (in this country) is usually too cool for comfort, and those seeking relaxation are likely to want to sit in a sunnier and warmer part of the garden. Plan No. 14 (opposite) is of a north-facing site with the ground sloping up from the house. The doors and windows look out on to a comparatively small paved area from which a way leads off to other parts of the garden.

The top right hand corner is a sun-trap and a level plateau has been made to form a circular paved area there, ringed with a wide grass verge, the total width being 20 feet (6m). On the side nearest the house the ground is retained by a wall, the top of which is level, or just below, the grass behind it and terminates in the natural slope at both ends. The plateau is perfectly flat and a comfortable place to arrange table and chairs with a view of the garden sloping away in three directions. A terrace is sometimes difficult to design, even if a level part of the garden is available, and to make it aesthetically acceptable and also functional a curved wall built in this way sometimes provides the solution.

The way up from the patio is by a gradual slope, partly grassed, with paving stones laid level with the lawn along the edge of the border. This provides a dry path to the terrace and plants near the front of the bed can sprawl at random without being damaged by the grass mower.

The design at the front of the house is one of extreme simplicity and it is based on a single curved line which embodies a paved section between the drive and front door. The approach to the house should I think have a look of welcome. All too often the emphasis is on the garage and the entrance to the front door is provided by a very secondary little path.

In this design the small front lawn is edged with low-growing shrubs which can be enjoyed by anyone waiting at the front door. Suitable shrubs for this sunnier part of the garden might include lavender (see p. 39) and *Lavatera olbia*.

Opposite: Plan 14 provides a place in the sun in a north-facing garden.

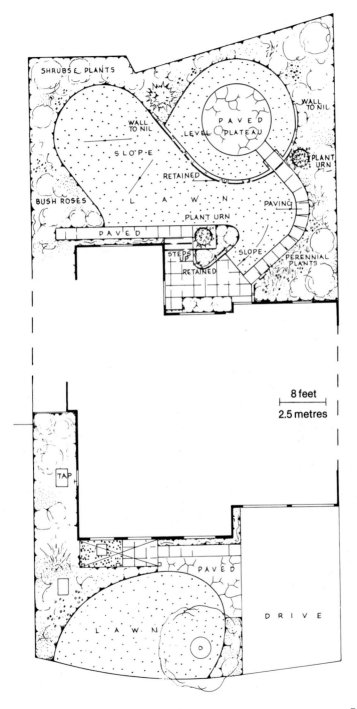

SHRUBS & PLANTS

WALL TO NIL

WALL TO NIL

PAVED LEVEL PLATEAU

PLANT URN

SLOPE

RETAINED

BUSH ROSES

L A W N

PAVING

PLANT URN

PAVED

STEPS UP

RETAINED

SLOPE

PERENNIAL PLANTS

8 feet
2.5 metres

TAP

PAVED

L A W N

D R I V E

Creating points of focal interest

The design in Plan No. 15 (opposite) is for a garden larger than the two preceding plots although it is a size typical of many gardens of today.

The outer sides of the garden are already constructed and the new cultivated sections consist of one fairly large island bed and another that is smaller. The design is again based on oblique lines and the feature of the garden is that it is possible to walk in different directions without seeing other parts at the same time.

The planting in the smaller island bed forms a substantial grouping of shrubs and balances similar elevations in the opposite border. This layout frames a view of a plant urn backed by a yew hedge in one direction and looking in the other there is a carefully chosen sculpture placed amongst bush roses, although it could equally well have been amongst the soft colours of herbaceous plants. Another view of the urn is between the existing border on the right side and the other straight side of the island bed, adding another dimension to the garden. It is the different aspects and association of line within a pattern of continuity that contributes to the overall design.

Erica herbacea 'Vivellii' forms dense hummocks.

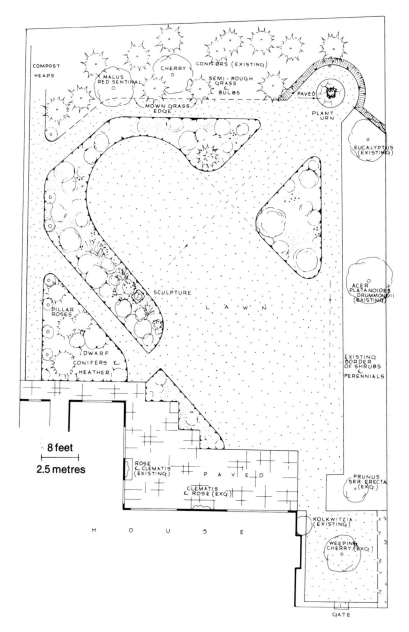

Plan 15. A garden incorporating several points of focal interest, for example an ornamental urn and a sculpture.

A rose garden

For the owner of a small garden roses are frequently grouped in separate beds or borders and contribute an abundance of blossom throughout the summer. Technically all roses are shrubs and many have found a permanent place in plant lists for mixed borders.

All the floribundas (cluster-flowered) are extremely useful in a mixed border of evergreen and deciduous shrubs and some perennial plants. The rose 'Queen Elizabeth' for example will tower 6 feet (1.8 m) or more at the back of the border; its counterpart 'Scarlet Queen Elizabeth', 'Iceberg' (white) and 'Chinatown' (yellow) are also roses for the back of the border. Nearer the front of the bed some shorter cultivars such as 'Elizabeth of Glamis', 'Intrigue' and 'Allgold' produce a succession of pink, crimson and yellow flowers, in bloom from June to October.

Hybrid tea roses (large-flowered) differ in that they rarely look comfortable in the mixed population of a shrub border, except perhaps certain very strong growers such as 'Buccaneer', 'Peace', 'Eden Rose' and 'Uncle Walter', and in fact it can be said that these plants, because of their size, are difficult to place in beds of shorter roses. In some rose gardens it is the practice to plant each bed with one colour and on a sufficiently large scale the effect is magnificent. When bush roses are part of the general layout, however, sometimes one of the most appropriate places for hybrid teas is within the lines of walls and paths where they help to create a semi-formal concept and do not look out of place.

Rose cultivars in the foreground near the house should not be tall growers because not only will the bushes obscure the view but the heights are out of scale for beds say 4 to 5 feet wide (1.2 to 1.5m). Different colours are often grown in the same bed and the most satisfactory result is usually obtained by planting groups of one colour and taking care to choose cultivars that are about equal in vigour.

Plan No. 16 (opposite) is for a rose garden of rather unconventional design occupying an area of about 80 by 30 feet (25 by 9m) – the size of many small gardens, although the plan shown is part of a larger garden with a secluded section for roses. A feature about the layout is that although it is effective as a rose garden it could also be taken as a design for a small ornamental garden and

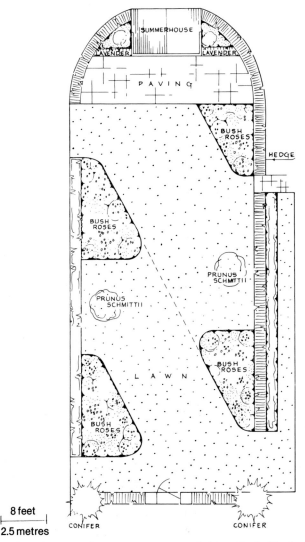

Plan 16: A rose garden of unconventional shape. Probably the best way to get ideas for rose borders is to visit the gardens of the Royal National Rose Society near St Albans.

instead of planting only roses, shrubs and perennials could also be grown. Whichever planting scheme is adopted the shape of the beds produces an enlarging effect on the garden and the actual clear space through the centre is 11 feet (3.3m) which will appear to elongate the distance to the summer-house from the gate. A similar effect looking from the other end, and the shaping of the beds, partially obscures sections of the grass in which two upright growing flowering cherry trees are planted. If all four are not devoted to roses two opposite sections could be planted with shrubs and perennials. Planted as a rose garden the beds are large enough to take enough bushes to give a good display of colour and one might be content to restrict the choice to four cultivars, or possibly as previously mentioned, several groups of different colours in each bed. The areas of blossom seen from eye-level will appear closer together than on the plan, because the view of the beds is foreshortened, so there is far less visible break between one bed and another producing a greater mass of colour from the paving in front of the summer-house and other parts of the garden.

'*Parkdirektor Riggers*', a climbing rose trained as a pillar.

Plant associations

A miscellaneous collection of shrubs and plants unrelated in colour or form cannot be expected to produce the effect of those that have been grouped with a sense of awareness that different plants are more congenial as neighbours than others, even although some are diverse in shape and character. The short list given below is offered as examples of plant associations and a brief description of combined colours and foliage textures.

1. *Cotinus coggygria* 'Notcutt's Variety', *Cornus alba* 'Elegantissima', *Senecio* 'Sunshine', *Ceratostigma willmottianum* and floribunda roses 'Dearest' or 'Arthur Bell'. Colours: deep purple foliage, grey-green and cream variegated leaves combined with grey-felted leaves, blue flowers, salmon pink or yellow roses; from early summer to late autumn. Red bark and grey leaves in the winter.

2. *Cortaderia selloana* 'Pumila', *Kniphofia uvaria, Salvia officinalis* 'Purpurascens'. Colours: grey-green arching leaves, silvery grey plumes with coral spikes, soft purple foliage, from summer to late autumn.

3. *Chamaecyparis lawsoniana* 'Columnaris', *Hebe rakaiensis.* Colours: glaucous blue and apple green leaves; all the year round.

4. *Taxus baccata* 'Standishii', *Lavandula spica* 'Hidcote'. Colours: golden foliage, grey leaves and purple flowers from mid-summer to autumn, evergreen foliage throughout the year.

5. *Kniphofia* 'Maid of Orleans', *Ceratostigma willmottianum, Anaphalis triplinervis, Hebe pinguifolia* 'Pagei'. Colours: cream, blue, white flowers, glaucous grey foliage; from early summer to late autumn.

6. *Fuchsia* 'Mrs Popple', *Calluna vulgaris* 'Alba Plena', *Campanula portenschlagiana* 'Major'. Colours: carmine and purple, white, blue; from early summer to late autumn.

7. *Potentilla fruticosa* 'Elizabeth', *Nepeta × faassenii.* Colours: primrose yellow, pastel-grey foliage, lavender blue flowers; from early summer to late autumn.

8. *Bergenia* (all cultivars), hardy ferns, *Vinca major* 'Elegantissima'. Colours: mainly foliage, large bottle green

or reddish bronze leaves, laciniate fronds, soft green edged with pale yellow variegated leaves, blue; from spring to late autumn.

9. *Cotinus coggygria* 'Notcutt's Variety', *Hippophae rhamnoides*. Colours: deep purple foliage, silver leaves, silver twigs, orange berries; from early summer to late autumn.

10. *Cotoneaster dammeri*, *Hebe albicans*, *H. rakaiensis*, *Ruta graveolens* 'Jackman's Blue'. Colours: deep green foliage, flowers white, berries red, glaucous leaves, apple green leaves, opalescent blue foliage.

11. *Forsythia* or *Chaenomeles*, *Pulmonaria angustifolia*. Colours: yellow or pink and blue flowers; early spring.

12. *Buddleja davidii* cultivars, *Erica* and *Calluna*. Colours: purple, pink; mid-summer to late autumn.

13. *Rhododendron* 'Britannia', *Saxifraga umbrosa*. Colours: ruby-red, foamy pale pink inflorescence; late spring.

14. Floribunda rose 'Iceberg' or hybrid musk rose 'Prosperity', *Senecio cineraria* 'White Diamond'. Colours: white, silver-grey foliage with blue and mauve flowers; early summer to late autumn.

15. *Hamamelis mollis*, *Erica carnea*. Colours: yellow, purplish pink; mid-winter to early spring.

16. *Corylus avellana* 'Contorta', *Erica herbacea*. Colours: yellow catkins, twisted branches, purplish pink flowers; mid-winter to early spring.

17. *Cotinus coggygria* 'Notcutt's Variety', *Hedera colchica* 'Variegata'. Colours: deep purple foliage, blue-green, soft yellow variegated leaves.

18. Floribunda rose 'Iceberg', *Lavandula spica* 'Hidcote', *Agapanthus* Headbourne Hybrids, *Nepeta* × *faassenii*. Colours: white, grey leaves, purple flowers, blue and lavender blue flowers.

19. *Cornus mas*, *Muscari*, *Erica herbacea*. Colours: yellow, blue, purplish pink; mid-winter to early spring.

20. *Phygelius capensis* 'Coccineus', *Ceratostigma willmottianum*, *Senecio* 'Sunshine'. Colours: scarlet, plumbago-blue, felted grey leaves.